This address, dealing with the history of Pepperdine Univer-
sity, was delivered at a "1981 Southern California Meeting"
of The Newcomen Society in North America held in Los
Angeles, when Dr. M. Norvel Young was the guest of
honor and speaker on November 2nd, 1981.

". . . Pepperdine University faces the changing future with the unchanging principle of faith in God and the potential of man."

—Dr. M. Norvel Young

Pepperdine University

A Place, A People, A Purpose

DR. M. NORVEL YOUNG

MEMBER OF THE NEWCOMEN SOCIETY
CHANCELLOR, PEPPERDINE UNIVERSITY
MALIBU, CALIFORNIA

THE NEWCOMEN SOCIETY IN NORTH AMERICA
NEW YORK   EXTON   PRINCETON   PORTLAND

1982

Newcomen Publication Number 1165

Library of Congress
Catalog Card Number 82-60566

Permission to abstract is granted
provided proper credit is allowed

The Newcomen Society, as a body,
is not responsible for opinions
expressed in the following pages

First Printing: August 1982

SET UP, PRINTED AND BOUND IN THE UNITED STATES
OF AMERICA FOR THE NEWCOMEN SOCIETY IN
NORTH AMERICA BY PRINCETON UNIVERSITY PRESS

INTRODUCTION OF DR. M. NORVEL YOUNG IN LOS ANGELES ON NOVEMBER 2ND, 1981, BY DR. HOWARD A. WHITE, PRESIDENT OF PEPPERDINE UNIVERSITY AND MEMBER OF THE SOUTHERN CALIFORNIA COMMITTEE IN THE NEWCOMEN SOCIETY IN NORTH AMERICA

My fellow members of Newcomen and guests:

I CONSIDER it a great privilege to introduce a man with whom I have worked for nearly a quarter of a century, a colleague and friend, a man widely known for his generous spirit and Christian conviction, a man who believes in the inestimable worth and potential of each human being. And a man whose name and allegiance are indelibly inscribed in the history of Pepperdine University. I am happy that The Newcomen Society is honoring him and Pepperdine University this evening.

In 1938, when George Pepperdine College was but one year old, a bright and energetic young educator fresh out of graduate school at Vanderbilt University accepted a teaching job in the social sciences at the fledgling Los Angeles institution named for its founder.

M. Norvel Young might describe those halcyon days at Pepperdine College as among the most dynamic in his life. As a member of the premier faculty of the new college, he accepted the challenge with eagerness and a deep sense of commitment, teaching students like Kenneth Hahn and Dean Olaf Tegner who would become pillars of our Los Angeles community.

He also met and married a Pepperdine coed named Helen Mattox, an alumna of the second graduating class, with whom he would share a lifelong career in independent higher education.

In 1941, the Youngs departed Pepperdine College for Nashville, Tennessee, Norvel's birthplace, where he completed work on his doctoral degree at George Peabody College. He turned his attentions to Christian service for some years, as a minister, a co-founder of Lubbock Christian College and as a trustee for nearly a decade at Abilene Christian University.

As if a Pepperdine College destiny were to guide his life, Dr. M. Norvel Young was beckoned in 1957 to become the third president of Pepperdine College upon the celebration of its twentieth anniversary. Still a small, unpretentious school in the Southern California

DR. HOWARD A. WHITE
PRESIDENT
PEPPERDINE UNIVERSITY

shadow of two towering educational giants, Pepperdine College had tapped Norvel Young to chart its progress into the decade of the Sixties. "Hope is faith in the future tense," he proclaimed, as he began to march the institution to national prominence.

He ignited the torch which illuminated that progress, developing an innovative academic master plan for both the liberal arts and professional programs. Graduate schools of business, education and professional studies were established. During his tenure as chief executive officer, enrollment swelled from 950 students to 7,500, and a single-campus college evolved amid the tempestuous and strife-torn Sixties into a multi-campus university by 1970. He became chancellor of the university in 1971, and is acknowledged as one of the principal architects of the dream that today is our 819-acre Malibu campus.

His wisdom, leadership and tenacity have brought a dynamic spirit to Pepperdine University which today is manifest in Frank R. Seaver College of Letters, Arts and Sciences; the Schools of Law, Business and Management, and Education; in three educational centers in Southern California; and in our Year-in-Europe program in Heidelberg, Germany.

M. Norvel Young has maintained a high profile in civic, educational and community endeavors. In 1970, he accepted the appointment of then-Governor Ronald Reagan to serve a four-year term on the Coordinating Council for Higher Education in California, representing all independent colleges and universities in the state, and is a longtime member of the American Association of Administrators of Colleges and Universities. He is the author of four books, a former editor and publisher and now chairman of the board of *20th Century Christian*, an active Rotarian and a former director of the Los Angeles Area Chamber of Commerce.

He has served the Los Angeles Philanthropic Foundation, is a founding member of the Board of Governors of the Los Angeles County Museum of Art, is a former vice president of the Museum of Natural History and is a member of numerous boards serving business and industry. Dr. Young was presented an honorary doctorate from the College of Physicians and Surgeons at the University of California at Irvine, and is a two-time recipient of the George Washington Medal from the Freedoms Foundation at Valley Forge.

A world traveler, a popular speaker and a dedicated family man, we may count among the many contributions of Dr. and Mrs. Young the four Young children, who themselves have distinguished careers in human service.

Members of Newcomen and guests, it is my pleasure to present Pepperdine University's third president and today its chancellor, DR. M. NORVEL YOUNG.

My fellow members of Newcomen, friends of Pepperdine University and special guests:

TONIGHT we celebrate the dynamic and colorful forty-four year history of Pepperdine University. It truly is a significant event when we consider the number of small, independent colleges and universities which have closed in the last five years or will close by the end of this decade. The *Los Angeles Times* recently forecast a 2.2 percent overall drop in enrollment among private colleges nationwide, due to a weakened economy, declining government support for education and rising tuition costs. But I am thrilled to be able to relate a success story of a very small, independent school which has grown into a thriving university in the State of California, a state which has the best-funded, tax-supported system of higher education in the history of civilization.

Pepperdine University and The Newcomen Society have much in common, for the university is a by-product of the American system of private enterprise. Its founder, George Pepperdine, in the true spirit of an entrepreneur, established the auto supply industry in the West. At the age of fifty, he founded Pepperdine College as a tangible expression of his spiritual value system. It is a story worth telling.

Pepperdine University grew out of the vision of a man born in a one-room cabin in the rich farmlands of Kansas in 1886. His youth was influenced by a deep religious commitment. He followed in the footsteps of his parents who were members of a frontier religious movement designed to restore Christianity as it was in the first century. Young George Pepperdine, after gaining a business college education, was first employed with a local gas company at a salary of six dollars a week.

If I might borrow a label currently in vogue, George Pepperdine was a *Venture Capitalist*. He had observed with curiosity that automobiles in 1906 were sold in a stripped condition; few came equipped with tops, windshields or bumpers, and if the owner were to have a headlight, he would have to purchase an oil-burning lamp and hang it on the front of the car. George pondered the possibility of establishing an auto parts business to fill an obvious need of the consumer. Newly married, he was faced with domestic obligations. His job as a bookkeeper at a Kansas City garage paid him a relatively comfortable fifteen dollars a week. That was security! But, George Pepperdine was a risktaker. He had five dollars and a good idea. The idea was that the horseless carriage needed additional parts.

His initial investment bought 500 penny postcards to advertise his new mail-order auto parts business to American automobile owners. (Perhaps we should have a moment of silence in our 20-cent-letter age in memory of the penny postcard and the two-cent letter.) George sent these cards listing retail prices to all car owners in the Kansas City area. When the cash orders came in he purchased the items from a wholesaler, wrapped them at home and mailed them. Thus, the huge Western Auto Supply chain was born.

Years later, George Pepperdine moved to California and started branch stores here. He successfully weathered the Depression and sold his business in 1939. By that date he had established one-hundred-seventy stores in eleven Western states with numerous associate stores selling Western Auto products.

When he realized he was a multi-millionaire at fifty, George Pepperdine felt a greater sense of responsibility to society. He had established a non-profit Eleemosynary Foundation in 1931 to provide gifts to religious, charitable and educational organizations. He gave generously to Churches of Christ, to the Y.M.C.A., to the Boy Scouts and established a girls' home. But he longed to do something more significant.

He considered the possibility of establishing a college. "I had seen young people go off to college with strong Christian faith and after four years, under the guidance of cynical and materialistic professors, return home minus their high ideals and faith in God," George Pepperdine was heard to have said. He had no intention of contributing his money to the founding of such an institution. If a college could be established which would provide a Christian environment, employ dedicated professors of scholarship with a profound faith in God, offer a sound curriculum which would reflect excellence in every area, be it business training, art, science or history, he was interested.

It was February of 1937. Mr. Pepperdine consulted a Los Angeles County school administrator, Hugh M. Tiner, who suggested that Dr. Batsell Baxter, the former president of Abilene Christian College and the current president of David Lipscomb College, be invited to come to Los Angeles and discuss the college concept. Dr. Baxter came to California, and in the course of his talks with George Pepperdine, asked the businessman what he wanted.

"That's the whole trouble, Dr. Baxter," replied George. "I don't know exactly what I want. I don't want another college that will be dependent upon the churches for support. I have in mind a privately endowed, four-year liberal arts college, an institution of higher learning where any worthy young person, regardless of his religion or financial standing, can get an education. And I want it to be a college that is academically sound, based on Christian faith. Is that too much to ask?"

George Pepperdine answered his own question. In the fall of 1937, announcement of the founding of the new college made the pages of *Time* magazine: "Last week George Pepperdine was bubbling with plans for a new enterprise to be called George Pepperdine College. He has thirty-four acres of land on Los Angeles' flat south side, and plans for ten buildings, of which four, low and glass-sided, will be ready for use this autumn. Mr. Pepperdine has already lined up a president, Batsell Baxter of Tennessee's David Lipscomb College, a faculty recruited from Duke, the University of Colorado, the University of California and several small Southern schools."

Several of us here tonight worked personally with Mr. and Mrs. Pepperdine in building the college. We are here because George Pepperdine drew us together with his noble dream.

Pepperdine College, whose acreage at 79th Street and Vermont Avenue was purchased for $150,000, was a brave new experiment launched in the midst of the Depression. There was a spirit of unbounded optimism among faculty, administrators and students. It was located in a bright, new, middle-class suburb, quite a distance by streetcar from downtown Los Angeles. There were no freeways. There was no war, although the war clouds in Europe were threatening. There were 167 eager students from many states. Department chairmen were paid an enviable $3,000 per year. There was a million-dollar endowment. George Pepperdine College gained <u>full</u> accreditation just seven months after its founding.

President Batsell Baxter made an impressive beginning. Then Hugh Tiner took the helm as president in 1939. When the postwar influx of GIs caused the college's enrollment to soar, every nook and cranny, including the basement of the president's home, was used for classroom space. Temporary buildings were moved to the campus. Apartments were erected quickly on a site known for years as Normandie Village. (There is nothing so permanent about a college as temporary buildings!)

Enrollment reached a peak of 1,590 students in 1948-49, and interest in sports and extracurricular programs surged. The Pepperdine "Waves" became the team to beat in basketball, baseball and tennis. Alumni were beginning to distinguish themselves in education, business and public service careers.

But as quickly as World War II veterans converged upon the campus, they disappeared upon graduation in 1953. Enrollment plummeted to a postwar low of 823 students that year, then began to climb again, inching up over 1,000 students by 1956. That same year, graduate study in the Department of Education was begun.

In 1957 it was a professional challenge for me to return as president to the college of my teaching roots. President Robert Hutchins of the University of Chicago once commented that to secure a college president you must find one capable of handling the position but foolish enough to accept it. I certainly had the second qualification. The challenge was before me. George Pepperdine met serious financial reverses and was no longer able to make any gifts to balance the budget.

Only half of the Pepperdine College operating budget was derived from tuition: the other fifty percent had to be obtained through endowment income, auxiliary enterprises and gifts. The original $1 million endowment had been seriously depleted by operating deficits. Salaries had not risen for several years. Maintenance had been deferred and the prospects for success were bleak.

But, the board was united and George Pepperdine and Don Miller, the chairman, were supportive. Bryant Essick, the chairman of the President's Board, an advisory board which Hugh Tiner had established, was encouraging. The first year we failed to balance the budget by $30,000. The second year we were in the black, and this year we celebrated our 25th consecutive year with a balanced budget.

This year, as a credit to President Howard A. White and his sound fiscal management, we had an operating budget of $45 million with

$2 million for endowment and plant renewal. We received an over-whelming vote of confidence with a record $12.4 million in gifts—the largest of any co-educational, independent university of our size and character in the nation.

We moved cautiously in the 1960s seeking to build a solid academic program. We pioneered the trimester schedule to use our classroom and office space year-round, and in 1963 we launched a Year-in-Europe program for undergraduates. The picturesque campus in Heidelberg, Germany was established under the directorship of Dr. Howard A. White, then chairman of the Department of History. Our graduate programs grew steadily, and in 1967 enrollment was at 1,500. We built a new dormitory on campus and enjoyed such good relations with our constituency that we attracted 14,000 participants for an annual series of lectures in the sports arena. George Pepperdine arrived in an ambulance. He enjoyed watching his college grow for more than a quarter century.

But, just when we thought things were looking up we experienced the Watts Riots in 1965. Our entire campus was in the curfew zone, and the National Guard occupied it for a control center. Our immediate neighborhood was supportive, but it became increasingly difficult to attract students to live in the area. In 1969 a neighborhood teenager was shot accidentally by a campus security officer. The situation was tense. The administration negotiated all night in the bedroom of the president's home to prevent the entire campus from being burned down in retaliation. One morning we found all the classroom buildings locked from the inside and a fire burning on the stage of the auditorium. The outlook was grim. I have thanked God many times that we did not have a "Kent State" confrontation.

Donors were reluctant to build buildings in such an atmosphere. In 1968 I appointed a committee of members of our President's Board to survey sites for a larger second campus with the idea of keeping our graduate and professional programs on the Los Angeles campus and moving the undergraduate programs to the new campus. At this time my mind went back to a young man whom I had identified when he graduated from David Lipscomb College in Nashville, Tennessee. His name was William S. Banowsky. He was obviously what we called in Tennessee "a five-gaited horse"—a man of many talents. At that time he was preaching in Lubbock, Texas. He had completed his doctoral work at the University of Southern California and had previously served as dean of students at Pepperdine. I asked him to consider assisting us in building a new campus.

Several years before, Frank Roger Seaver, president of the international oil tool firm, the Hydril Company, had begun to help Pepperdine. I will never forget the first time Vice President William Teague and I asked him to help on a film project illustrating the difference between Communism and the private enterprise system. Henry Salvatori had recommended that we visit Mr. Seaver. We asked his help on a $15,000 project. We were seeking 15 people to give $1,000 each. Instead he wrote out a check for $7,500 and, with a grin, handed it to me saying, "Do you think this will help?" It not only helped, it put the project over the top. We obtained additional support from Richard M. Scaife of Pittsburgh. With this assistance we launched a series of freedom seminars and summer programs for public school teachers. The sowing of this seed brought an abundant harvest. It wasn't popular then to be "Conservative" or patriotic or even "anti-Communist," but we dared to be different.

Our site selection committee looked at more than forty locations that were available, but the choice finally narrowed to three: acreage in Westlake Village, a location in Palos Verdes and the Malibu site, offered by the historic Frederick Hastings Rindge family. Mrs. Frank Roger Seaver had already pledged $1 million and was offering a beautiful site in Palos Verdes overlooking the ocean.

When Dr. Banowsky accepted the challenge to join in building our new campus, I introduced him to Mrs. Seaver. Together, we drove to the Palos Verdes site. Most of the sites that had been offered required that we build upon them in order to receive the gift. She was interested in the purposes of the institution and offered to make her gift with the understanding that the University could sell the land and use the proceeds to build on one of the other two sites. Both Dr. Banowsky and I fell in love with Malibu and did our best to persuade the site selection committee and the trustees that we should accept this generous offer of 138 prime acres in the midst of Malibu. Some of the trustees were concerned about the cost of developing this mountainous land, but we obtained a special gift from Mr. Scaife to provide for the extra cost of building on the Malibu site. He was strongly in favor of this location, and through the years has given over $10 million toward the project; without his assistance our spectacular Malibu campus would not have become a reality.

We promised Merritt Adamson, Sylvia Rindge Neville and Rhoda-May Adamson Dallas, three of the grandchildren of Frederick Hastings Rindge, that we would raise at least $6 million to build a branch campus on the new site in Malibu. Frederick Hastings Rindge had moved to Malibu in 1891 and bought more than 13,000 acres for as much as $10 an acre. His descendants had long wanted to use this particular setting for something significant. We are extremely indebted to them, as we are to Mrs. Frank Roger Seaver who pledged $8 million in stock to enable us to build the Frank Roger Seaver College of Letters, Arts and Sciences.

Mrs. Seaver and her nephew, Richard, now president of Hydril Company, immediately recognized the remarkable talents of Dr. Banowsky. Together we began to plan for a small but significant college of high academic standards which would adhere to its historic Christian roots. Frank Seaver and Blanche Seaver already had made unprecedented gifts to California higher education at Pomona College, Loyola University, the University of Southern California and other institutions. She now decided that she would honor her husband by carrying out the great dream which they had shared: to build a liberal arts college of academic excellence, founded upon the principles of private enterprise and loyalty to God and country.

The site selection committee's goal presented a challenge to the university: before the buildings were built, we would be sure to design the best program possible to be housed in them. An abundance of small seminar-type rooms were planned with a complement of audio-visual aides and library carrels in addition to the traditional faculty lecture facilities. Extensive studies were conducted to determine what the great universities and the small independent colleges were doing, so that the best might be incorporated into the new program. At the same time, the college retained the nationally recognized architectural firm of William L. Pereira and Associates, which incorporated the decisions of the curriculum committee with the practicality and the realities of the physical site. We wanted to make both curriculum and buildings blend together harmoniously to create an overall atmosphere of exciting originality. There were those who wanted us to build on the flat meadow; but at considerable expense, the costlier but quality choice was made to build in the mountains overlooking the meadow.

It was time to let the public know of our dreams! Plans were formulated to unveil the architectural drawings and to announce "the birth of a college." Faculty, alumni and friends were invited to a gala event at the Century Plaza Hotel. Reservations flooded in, overflowing the ballroom, so arrangements were made to simultaneously use the International Ballroom of the Beverly Hilton Hotel. Governor Ronald Reagan spoke at both hotels, shuttling back and forth in the rain. Mr. Scaife of Pittsburgh, Mrs. Frank Roger Seaver and Richard Seaver, Fritz Huntsinger, Leonard Firestone, George Elkins, Mrs. B. D. Phillips, the John Tylers, Mrs. Margaret Martin Brock, Morris Pendleton, the Charles Paysons of New York, Clint Murchison of Dallas, Jerene Appleby Harnish, the John Stauffers, Bill and Bob Ahmanson and a host of others joined us that evening of February 9, 1970. William Pereira unveiled the dramatic campus plans, and we launched the new undergraduate college with a $24.5-million campaign. It was an auspicious beginning.

Ground-breaking ceremonies took place on the Malibu campus on May 23, 1970. *U.S. News and World Report* editor David Lawrence offered the keynote address on "The Role of the Private College in Today's World." As he stressed the diversity of the public and private educational sectors he noted, "Moral force has not yet reached the high point in our country or in the world, but certainly our colleges can contribute a great deal to its development, and private colleges have a special opportunity in this pursuit." And so at this juncture in our nation's history when college campuses were torn with the strife of riots and revolts, when students were being jailed and killed, Pepperdine University countered the tide in establishing a new campus dedicated to moral and spiritual values, to conservative patriotism as well as to academic excellence. This was the beginning of an exciting and historic chapter in California independent higher education.

But the dawn of the Seventies was a tense era in higher education. Governor Ronald Reagan could not attend the Regents Meeting at the University of California without extensive police protection. In the face of disapproval of many campuses, Pepperdine dared to confer upon him its highest award, the Honorary Doctor of Laws degree.

President Reagan has ascended the Pepperdine dais on seven occasions since that inaugural dinner. He is a founding member of the Pepperdine University Associates. His encouragement to the university has been a great factor in our success.

In 1971, Pepperdine College became Pepperdine University. Later that year, Dr. William S. Banowsky became president and I became chancellor of the university. More than $36 million had been raised by this time to begin construction of the marvelous Malibu campus.

The Frank R. Seaver College of Letters, Arts and Sciences of Pepperdine University opened in the fall of 1972. It was an exciting time. Bill Banowsky used to remark in his many speeches, as we were raising funds and moving mountains, that we could do anything that God and Mrs. Frank Roger Seaver agreed upon, and not necessarily in that order.

Attorney Joseph Bentley of the firm of Latham and Watkins, who has been our legal counsel for many years, is convinced that Pepperdine University has a manifest destiny. Many others agree in calling our emergence the "miracle of Malibu." There is evidence of that. For example, Mr. Bentley notes the fact that Seaver College opened for business the first week of September 1972, just days before the September 21 "Friends of Mammoth Decision"—regarding an environmental impact report—was handed down by the California Supreme Court. If this "Friends of Mammoth" case had occurred just a few days earlier it would have substantially delayed the opening of the campus and greatly increased the cost. Exactly 60 days after the campus opened, the California Coastal Zone Conservation Act of 1972 was adopted. If it had been adopted any earlier it would have drastically curtailed the development of the campus as we know it today.

As Mr. Bentley says, even more dramatic than the fortuitous timing of these events was the amazing failure of an attempted appeal from the Regional Commission's issuance of a coastal permit for a new sewage disposal system. The permit was issued June 13, 1977, by a 10 to 1 vote. The opponents had until 5 p.m. of the tenth working day after the decision of the Regional Commission to appeal. On June 27, 1977, the tenth working day, Joe Bentley called the State Coastal Commission just before 5 p.m. and was informed that a telegram and telephone call had been received from the opposition, but that neither was adequate under the regulations. They had failed

DR. M. NORVEL YOUNG
CHANCELLOR
PEPPERDINE UNIVERSITY

to name all the persons who spoke at the regional public hearing. The next day, Mr. Bentley learned that at 5:15 p.m. the previous day, a completed and proper appeal had arrived on the prescribed form, but had been declared untimely and void. The following day an exact copy arrived by mail, but was again refused. If we had not obtained this permit, we could not have sold our CEFA bond issue the next month and it could have resulted in the closing of the campus or a postponement of the construction of the Law School, the Fine Arts Building and additional student housing.

Joe Bentley says there have been so many "coincidences" that he is convinced that Pepperdine has a manifest destiny. Surely the past is prologue. A recent study made by the educational consulting firm of Brakeley, John Price Jones, Inc., found that the faculty, staff and Board of Pepperdine University have "an excitement created by a sense of destiny."

The formal dedication of the Frank R. Seaver College of Letters, Arts and Sciences was celebrated on April 20, 1975, with Ronald Reagan dedicating the campus before 2,000 people crowded into the Fouch Amphitheatre on campus. President Banowsky spoke in tribute:

> Five years ago on May 25, 1970, as we broke the first ground for Seaver College on our Malibu Campus, we pledged to bring together a community of scholars who hold distinctive spiritual beliefs. In 1938, George Pepperdine chose for the motto of this university a verse of scripture from the Book of Matthew, "Freely you have received, freely give." No person has more powerfully believed that truth than Blanche Ellen Theodora Ebert Seaver. Her maiden name, Theodora, is of Greek derivation meaning 'the gift of God.' I believe it is within the providence of God that Mrs. Seaver was brought into our lives. A college is, after all, something like a human being in that both must have a soul of some kind. My deepest concern and desire of dedication is for the soul of Seaver College. I would like in the final analysis for our work to be judged on the basis of what we believe and how we put that faith into action.

Under President Banowsky's leadership, Seaver College became the very heart of the university, around which the graduate and professional schools are clustered. Enrollment at Seaver College has been limited to 2,100 full-time students, most of whom reside in residential housing on the campus. The faculty is devoted to the development of the whole person—physical, mental, social and spiritual. The fine and performing arts as well as a comprehensive intercollegiate sports program for undergraduate students enhance the basic core of general education requirements. Seaver College is truly the flagship of our 7,000-student university.

President Banowsky closed his California chapter and his seven-year term as the university's chief executive officer on September 15, 1978, to assume the presidency of the University of Oklahoma. He said in a televised interview, "Few people in Southern California can now realize and appreciate that Pepperdine University will be one of the best-endowed institutions in the American West in a few short years. That reality has been assured us and I am glad to leave when the stock is high."

But our stock continued to rise. The man who was chosen to be the fifth president of the university was the man whom Dr. Banowsky had selected to serve as executive vice president and to run the institution internally during his tenure, Dr. Howard A. White. We salute Dr. White tonight for sustaining the momentum and for being the man most responsible for consolidating and improving the academic programs of the university.

He is a dedicated scholar, author and executive, highly esteemed by his colleagues both within and outside the university. The academic progress for which he is largely responsible at Pepperdine University did not go unnoticed in the news media. In a 1978 story, the Los Angeles Times stated that "Pepperdine University is in a class by itself. . . . Its main campus has become a glittering diamond set on 650 acres at Malibu. The sparkle runs deep, and to many observers it symbolizes the University's academic progress."

Under President White's guidance, the university has focused its attention on improving faculty salaries, and next year the university will rank in the top division of faculty salaries as ranked by the American Association of University Professors. It is also heartening to review statistics on the percentage of faculty members who possess the earned doctorate. In the California State University system 75 percent of the faculty hold the earned doctorate. Among faculty of the University of California it is 90 percent. Among the state's private colleges and universities, 60 percent of the faculty hold the doctorate or its equivalent. At Pepperdine University, 91 percent possess the earned doctorate or its equivalent.

Pepperdine University's 7,000 students hail from 50 states and 65 countries. Enrollment limits enable the university to select top candidates from a growing pool of applicants. For example, during the 1980-81 academic year, the university received 28,841 letters of inquiry from high school students nationwide and more than 10,000 from foreign countries. While the national average of scholastic aptitude scores has continued to decline over the last four years, averages for incoming freshmen at Seaver College have risen by 64 points. Seaver College enrolls only those students who exhibit potential and promise for academic success.

Although President White has concentrated on upgrading faculty salaries, the standards of admission and the quality of teaching, he has not neglected the physical plant expansion program. More than $25 million in student and faculty facilities are under construction at the present time. In its issue of October 26, 1981, *The Wall Street Journal* reported on our 50-unit faculty/staff housing project and commended the university for creating affordable housing to attract and retain good faculty. The NBC "Today" show complimented our vision in providing faculty housing on campus.

One of our goals is to attract faculty who have already made their mark in research and teaching excellence and who would like to extend their professional career at Pepperdine. With this housing program, we find great interest from faculty at the nation's top institutions who would like to pursue their teaching careers on our campus of 819 acres—smog-free, sun-kissed, ocean-washed, island-girded and mountain-guarded. Our music building, part of the Ahmanson Fine Arts Center, is scheduled for completion in 1982, and the Helen Field Heritage Hall adjacent to the Firestone Fieldhouse is due for occupancy in early 1983.

One of the secrets of Pepperdine's phenomenal growth has been the camaraderie and unity of philosophy of a capable and dynamic administrative team. Among them, none has worked harder nor more effectively in fund raising than our Vice Chancellor Charles Runnels.

Men like Dr. Runnels and Vice President for University Affairs James Wilburn are responsible for a large measure of Pepperdine's success.

In addition to the university's flagship, Seaver College, the three professional schools—the School of Law, the School of Business and Management and the Graduate School of Education—are growing with new academic centers in Irvine, Sherman Oaks and El Segundo, adjacent to the Los Angeles airport. President White has recently completed the sale of the Los Angeles campus, originally purchased in 1937 for $150,000 and sold recently for $14 million. He is quite an entrepreneur himself!

George Pepperdine, an astute businessman, stressed business training for our students. Our School of Business and Management, which was founded in 1970, administers the third largest graduate business program in the nation. More than 2,500 students, the majority of whom are working adults with full-time careers, are currently studying for the master's degree. The median age of our graduate business students is 32 for men and 34 for women. Female degree candidates comprise 30 percent of our MBA student body.

We have enjoyed a great measure of success in the School of Business in bringing together an optimum mix of academic and real-world experience among our business faculty. Most of our professors have held top management positions with leading firms, some operate their own successful enterprises and others are consultants and authors. Among the School's students, 47 percent have the support of their companies in paying for their tuition. We like to think that Pepperdine pioneered the Executive MBA Program for top level administrators. We call it the Presidential/Key Executive MBA Program, from whose ranks have graduated more than 200 company presidents. We have no group of alumni more loyal or enthusiastic than those of our School of Business and Management. We confidently expect to underwrite a beautiful, functional, management conference center in the future with the support of our alumni.

Our School of Education is our oldest graduate program. William Johnston, former superintendent of the Los Angeles City schools, recently wrote to President White congratulating the university on the 34 years of close cooperation with the Los Angeles City schools in the preparation of teachers. Today, 2,000 Pepperdine University alumni are teaching in the Los Angeles Unified School District. In spite of the oversupply of teachers, there are never enough good ones, and our graduates are in demand, not only locally but across the nation. Our administrative internship program with the Los Angeles School District is the first program of its kind in California. Dean Olaf Tegner and his faculty are proud of a school that prepares teachers who care about their students and who are determined to help them fulfill their potential, whether in urban or suburban districts.

The School of Law, which shares the Malibu campus with Seaver College, has its roots in Orange County. Founded in 1964 as the Orange University College of Law, it was acquired by the university in 1969, and moved to its permanent facility on the Malibu campus in 1978. The School of Law is on the list of law schools approved by the American Bar Association, holds membership in the Association of American Law Schools and is fully accredited by the Committee of Bar Examiners.

Gifts from benefactors Jerene Appleby Harnish and Odell McConnell were principally responsible for the spectacularly beautiful and functional $6-million Odell McConnell Law Center on its 30-acre promontory 700 feet above the ocean.

The Law School maintains a restricted enrollment of 570 full-time students, admitting one student among every eight applicants. In addition to the three-year program of study leading to the juris doctor degree, we have a program in Great Britain to acquaint selected senior students with international law. Dean Ronald Phillips, the founding dean, takes seriously George Pepperdine's words that "If we educate a man's mind, but do not educate his heart, we make a dangerous man." Pepperdine's School of Law stressed ethical education long before Watergate. We also endorsed the private enterprise spirit of competition. At last year's national Moot Court competition, our Pepperdine team placed second in the nation. The first-place award eluded our School of Law team by only a fraction of a percentage point, after we beat a tenacious Harvard Law School team on the way to the final competition.

But the past is prologue. As we look to the future under the dynamic leadership of our fifth president, we face the kind of paradox that Richard Atkinson of the National Science Foundation describes. He says, "It is difficult for a university to be both conservative and innovative." We must be open to new ideas, yet conserve the integrity and the essential purpose of our founder. It is our mission to realize, uphold and defend the manifest destiny that is Pepperdine University, preserving the heritage of the ideals of this institution, its people, its purpose. As we stress teaching, we do not want to neglect research; as we stress the academic, we do not want to neglect the moral, ethical and spiritual; as we enjoy the fruits of a well-managed institution where the faculty reviews each fellow member every five years under our innovative tenure system, we do not want to rest on our laurels and fail to continue aggressively to seek outstanding new faculty. As we enjoy the beauty of our campus, we must be aware that beauty is merely a setting for achievement. One major supporter has defined Pepperdine's program as "a quest for excellence inherent in an educational setting, flavored by religious principles and patriotism." Another has said, "Pepperdine doesn't seem to carry the image of a church school, but rather it is a university with religious principles. This is a subtle distinction, but it is very important."

As we hold fast to our original mission to meet today's challenges, we move resolutely into the computer age. Jean-Jacques Servan-Schreiber, author of the best-selling book, *The World Challenge* and one of the most distinguished citizens of France, states that he sees Pepperdine as "the right place to be in the computer revolution." His son, Emile, is a freshman at Seaver College. We have launched an innovative computer literacy program that will offer professional growth experiences to administrators across the country. Thirty education leaders will be involved in a week-long seminar next summer. By the time Pepperdine is fifty years old, 75 percent of all jobs in the United States will require a knowledge of or use of computers. We want our students to be prepared.

And so, Pepperdine University faces the changing future with the unchanging principle of faith in God and the potential of man. We are dedicated to providing the best academic, cultural and spiritual context for our students, confident that these can play a vital part in our nation's future and the world's. President White shared this vision in his inaugural address:

Pepperdine University and Seaver College are very special because of the distinctive goals and purposes to which they are dedicated. We gladly proclaim our allegiance and our loyalty to these distinctive features of being—because with all of our hearts we believe that our beloved country and our world needs this kind of institution. Pepperdine University is so strongly established—its friends and supporters so numerous—its faculty so dedicated and financial resources so great; its heritage so valuable, and its distinctive purposes so needed in our society that its future, with the help of God, is bound to be one of glorious achievement.

When Daniel Webster was defending his alma mater, Dartmouth College, before the Supreme Court, he expressed the feeling of so many friends of Seaver College and Pepperdine University: "It's a small college, sirs, but there are those who love her."

THE END

"Actorum Memores simul affectamus Agenda!"

Pepperdine University Affirms

THAT GOD IS

That He is revealed uniquely in Christ

That the educational process may not, with impunity,
be divorced from the divine process

That the student, as a person of infinite dignity,
is the heart of the educational enterprise

That the quality of student life
is a valid concern of the University

That truth, having nothing to fear from investigation,
must be pursued relentlessly in every discipline

That spiritual commitment, tolerating no excuse
for mediocrity, demands the highest standards of
academic excellence

That freedom, whether spiritual, intellectual,
or economic, is indivisible

That knowledge calls, ultimately,
for a life of service

PEPPERDINE UNIVERSITY'S STATEMENT OF AFFIRMATION CAPTURES THE ESSENCE OF
THE UNIVERSITY'S UNIQUE MISSION